ITALY
Florence & Rome

Name · Date · Group

Cheyenne Protsman

6-18-2015

~ Rome to Geneva ~
Douglas Bond Tour

THE CHRISTIAN'S TRAVEL JOURNAL FOR ITALY

By Mario Mammina

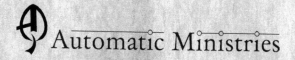

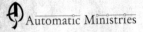
Automatic Ministries

The Christian's Travel Journal for Italy

First Edition 2014–2015

By Mario Mammina

Unless otherwise noted, all Scripture quotations are taken from the NEW AMERICAN STANDARD BIBLE®, © Copyright 1960, 1962, 1963, 1968, 1971, 1972, 1973, 1975, 1977, 1995 by The Lockman Foundation. Used by permission. www.Lockman.org.

Scripture quotations marked NLT are taken from the Holy Bible, New Living Translation, copyright 1996, 2004. Used by permission of Tyndale House Publishers, Inc., Wheaton, Illinois 60189. All rights reserved.

Scripture quotations marked MSG are taken from The Message. Copyright © 1993, 1994, 1995, 1996, 2000, 2001, 2002. Used by permission of NavPress Publishing Group.

Photography from Mario Mammina, Antonio Di Lisio, and Antonella Viglione

Background: Yellow Parchment Paper Antique © Can Stock Photo Inc. / rustyphil

ISBN: 978-1-940712-00-0 (Paperback)
ISBN: 978-1-940712-01-7 (eBook)

To Melanie:

My favorite travel companion and best friend.

INTRODUCTION

If including Christ in your vacation plans is a new concept, you have no idea what you've been missing.

A vacation presents the perfect opportunity to deepen your relationship with Jesus. You could return home from your trip with more than a few cheap souvenirs. You could be transformed.

The Christian's Travel Journal for Italy is designed to keep you engaged in your relationship with Christ as you experience one of the most beautiful countries in the world.

Journal Layout

Most guidebooks offer basic historical data. *The Christian's Travel Journal for Italy* supplements these books by sharing stories behind the history, linking them to truths found in Scripture, and connecting them with real-life applications.

Each chapter focuses on a different historical site and introduces facts you won't find in a traditional guidebook. At the end of each chapter are two Action Points that will help you apply the lessons learned so you won't forget your experience.

The Journal section provides prompts and blank space to help you document your thoughts and activities each day.

If you are a Christian, this journal will enable you to engage more fully with the One who made everything you are about to experience. It can help you grow closer to your travel companions and to Christ.

If you aren't sure whether or not you know Jesus, I invite you to read the Reality chapter at the end of the book. I pray you will make Jesus the Lord of your life every single day and night—whether on vacation or at home. It's the most important decision you'll ever make.

HOW TO USE THE JOURNAL

I recommend taking this journal with you to every site you visit and reading each story before and/or during your experience there. The journal is thin enough to fit in your back pocket.

Write in it daily, attach and add your thoughts to its pages, and you will have a keepsake of life changing memories to look back on for years to come.

I hope this book will edify your soul and accelerate your relationship with Jesus as you visit one of the most beautiful countries on the planet. May you return from your trip revived, deepened, and transformed.

Buon viaggio!

TABLE OF CONTENTS

FLORENCE

Souvenirs › Stamps › Notes

Santa Maria del Fiore

Piazza Del Duomo, 1 50122 Firenze
AD 1420-1436

Filippo Brunelleschi hated losing—especially to his long-time artistic competitor, Lorenzo Ghiberti. Both Brunelleschi and Ghiberti were finalists to sculpt the bronze doors of the Baptistery of San Giovanni, next to Florence's cathedral, Santa Maria del Fiore. The sculptors stood beside their work, anxiously waiting for thirty-four judges to decide the winner. The victor would receive showers of praise and never have to worry about finding jobs again.

The judges revealed the results. Brunelleschi had lost.

With clenched fists, a crushed heart, and shattered self-confidence, Brunelleschi stormed away from the baptistery and left for Rome. His sojourn would last as long as it took for the echoes of the cheers for his rival to fade away. Brunelleschi swore to never work in bronze again.

For the next fifteen years, Brunelleschi returned to his roots as a clockmaker to earn enough to survive and cultivate a passion for the ancient Roman ruins. He spent most of his time digging through the rubble and studying centuries-old vaulting techniques. One particular building, the Pantheon, taught him the most. Within its concrete dome, a new inspiration dawned inside him.

News of another competition brought his ideas to full light. The Santa Maria del Fiore, the half-completed cathedral in Florence, needed a dome. It would be the largest in the world. The winning design would require the artist to defy gravity. Brunelleschi must have smiled when he realized the size of the shadow such a dome would cast on the Baptistery of San Giovanni.

For years the Florentines had prayed for God to send them someone who could achieve a feat that most people called impossible. In the previous hundred years, several architects had been hired by the cathedral and all failed to complete the task.

Even Ghiberti tried his hand and fell short.

Brunelleschi accepted the challenge, took what he had learned from the Pantheon, and constructed the dome.

If Brunelleschi had won the competition for the bronze baptistery doors, he might never have traveled to Rome. And he would not have possessed the knowledge to build the dome.

Brunelleschi's dome reminds us why we can't let discouragement and blind-side moments crush us.

Failure makes us realize our need for God's help. This produces humility. Brunelleschi learned how to construct a dome, not at the peak of his career, but in the valley, when he was humbled. We are most moldable when our pride is diminished.

God's timing trumps everything—even our abilities. We may be great at something, but our achievements will never out-win God's timing. Brunelleschi made great doors at the competition, but God had bigger plans for him.

God, the Master Builder, used a defeated man, who lived in the valley of brokenness, to revolutionize architecture and engineering forever. Just like Brunelleschi, we need to allow our discouragements to transform into humility so God can mold us. We must be patient and wait on Him to raise us up so that we may glorify Him.

Action Point #1

Are you discouraged about something right now? Humble yourself before God. Admit you need His help. Ask Him to mold you into who He wants you to be for His time and His purpose. Remember to glorify Him.

Action Point #2

Have you traveled through a time of discouragement? Praise God for what you learned. Apart from Him, you can do nothing (Philippians 4:13). Climb the steps to the top of the dome—all 463 of them—and recall what God has taught you during your ascent. When you reach the top, thank Him again.

"Therefore, humble yourselves under the mighty hand of God, that He may exalt you at the proper time, casting all your anxiety on Him, because He cares for you" (1 Peter 5:6-7).

Souvenirs › Stamps › Notes

Michelangelo's David

L'Accademia · Via Ricasoli, 66 50122 Firenze

AD 1501

Rejected. No good. Unwanted. Unworkable. These are the types of words artists used to describe a rejected piece of marble from the mountains of Carrara. That is, until a twenty-six-year-old master sculptor took matters into his own hands. Literally. He shaped the rock under his hammer and chisel.

Michelangelo saw something in the raw stone others didn't see. "In every block of marble I see a statue as plain as though it stood before me, shaped and perfect in attitude and action. I have only to hew away the rough walls that imprison the lovely apparition to reveal it to the other eyes as mine see it."[1]

Michelangelo brought forth *David* from the rock. He took something rejected and made it extraordinary. The five-hundred-year-old, seventeen-foot statue still stands today in near-perfect detail, reflecting its master's talent.

We can pinpoint times in our lives when we felt like that rejected piece of marble—totally lost about who we were deep inside. But one day a Master took us and freed us.

God knew us before we were born. If anyone could

work on our internal, it had to be someone who knew us intricately—as plain as though we stood before Him.

Unlike Michelangelo, who passed away and left imperfections on *David*, our Master is still very much alive and continues to work on us—filing us down, sanding us to perfection. When we see Him face-to-face in heaven, His work will be complete. Until then, let's be like *David*—a moldable reflection of our Master for the entire world to see.

Action Point #1

You are God's masterpiece! Without Him, you are a block of rejected marble, attempting to free yourself so you can figure out who you really are. But like *David*, you cannot free yourself without a master sculptor. Have you asked God to free you?

Action Point #2

As you look at *David*, think about how God has freed you, shaped you, and molded you. Give Him thanks for being the Master of your life. Commit to allowing Him to continue the process until the days He numbered for you are completed.

> "For I am confident of this very thing, that He who began a good work in you will perfect it until the day of Christ Jesus" (Philippians 1:6).

"For we are His workmanship, created in Christ
Jesus for good works, which God prepared before-
hand so that we would walk in them"
(Ephesians 2:10).

Souvenirs › Stamps › Notes

Baptistery

After laboring over the same project for more than twenty years, Lorenzo Ghiberti stepped back from the masterpiece to admire his finished work. His bronze doors hung on the east side of the Baptistery of San Giovanni, the most trafficked side by the Florentines entering and exiting the Duomo. All ten panels depicting the Old Testament shimmered in the morning sun.

We may never know Lorenzo's temptation to validate the years of his hard labor. But fifty years later, Michelangelo spoke for Ghiberti. He coined the doors as fit to "grace the very gates of Paradise."[2] To this day, the name remains: *The Gates of Paradise*.

What if those words had come from Ghiberti's mouth instead of Michelangelo's? Would the praise have the same impact five hundred years later? Probably not. When someone praises himself, the achievement is spoiled. This turns the greatest success into another average accomplishment.

The praise came from Michelangelo, the one who sculpted *David,* and his praise brought power and validation to Ghiberti's work. If you look up Ghiberti's bronze doors in any guidebook or article, you will find Michelangelo's famous compliment mentioned within the first few paragraphs.

We must let others validate our accomplishments. Actually, the only approval that should matter is God's. After all, He gave us the talents we possess. Therefore, any praise we receive is ultimately His.

On the flip side, even if nobody validates us, we need to remember that there's One who sees what we've done. And He's the only one in the world worth impressing.

Action Point #1

Think about a time when you did something and told others of your greatness. Did your boasting decrease the impact of your accomplishment?

Action Point #2

Think about how you can compliment someone else. Be someone's Michelangelo today.

"Let another praise you, and not your own mouth;
a stranger, and not your own lips"
(Proverbs 27:2).

Souvenirs › Stamps › Notes

Uffizi Gallery
Via Della Ninna, 5 50122 Firenze
AD 1581

Because of the generosity of one woman, the Uffizi Gallery is one of the best museums in the world. Anna Maria Luisa de' Medici was the last of the Medici family. Some believe she saved Florence because she donated more than three centuries of collected artwork to the gallery.

Few museums come close to packing such an all-star lineup of artwork. Leonardo da Vinci, Giotto, Botticelli, Michelangelo, Raphael, and Caravaggio are among those featured.

What if Anna Maria had held on to this artwork and stored it somewhere safe? Or sold her precious collection for money? The artwork would be scattered all over the world and this museum wouldn't be near as popular—and possibly neither would Florence.

Do you own things that could bring joy and happiness to others if you were to give them away? Rather than collect dust in your closet or lint in your pocket, perhaps your possessions could be used to create a smile or give someone hope. Nothing we have belongs to us anyway. All our stuff is God's, including the intangibles, such as talents, time, and temperament. For whatever reason, He chose to put certain things in our possession. The question is, what are we going to do with what He's given us?

Few things in life are certain, but there's one truth that applies to all of us. The things we possess, no matter how precious they are, cannot come with us when we die.

Look for ways to give. Even if the things you possess are priceless. Even if all you have to give is your time. Or a smile. Or a touch. God has been generous, and so should we.

Action Point #1

As you walk through the museum, imagine that all these pieces of art are yours. You would be rich! But remember, you can't take even one euro with you when you die. Think about what priceless things you have back at home. What could you do with them?

Action Point #2

Give someone something of yours today. Buy a stranger a gelato or give a friend something you think he'd enjoy. See how addictive giving can be.

"Do not store up for yourselves treasures on earth, where moth and rust destroy, and where thieves break in and steal" (Matthew 6:19).

"But store up for yourselves treasures in heaven,
where neither moth nor rust destroys, and where
thieves do not break in or steal: for where your
treasure is, there your heart will be also"
(Matthew 6:20-21).

Souvenirs › Stamps › Notes

Ponte Vecchio

Ponte Vecchio, Firenze
AD 1345

Of all the bridges in Europe, this one tops the charts. Only when it's snowing or after midnight is this bridge empty of people. The silver and gold stores that line the bridge are a definite upgrade compared to the butcher shops that used to be in their place. Imagine the smell of leftover raw meat tossed into the River Arno on a hot day.

The Medici family, the richest in Italy during the Renaissance, had the bridge converted. After all, how could royalty be expected to walk among anything less than precious metals? The Medicis also commissioned Giorgio Vasari to add a corridor on top of the shops.

The walkway above the shops runs along the north riverbank and connects to the Uffizi Gallery. Going south, the corridor passes through Santa Felicita Church and into the Pitti Palace. This corridor served as a passageway for the prominent Medici family so they could walk from the palace to their offices, where they governed the city.

Every day the Medicis walked above the river Arno, and the Florentines, on a bed of silver and gold. Even the part of the corridor built through the church opened up to a private balcony that separated the family from others during worship. This lifestyle allowed the Medicis to live their lives without ever having to interact with the common people.

Sometimes we wish we had a personal corridor where we could go from point A to point B each day without the need to interact with others. But that's the opposite of what Jesus exemplified. He laid aside all the glory due Him and reduced Himself to be the lowest among us.

When we consider what He did, our perspective changes, and we no longer desire our own corridor. Even walking *among* people isn't enough. Jesus walked *with* people. We must do the same, even when others "block our view" or get in the way. Jesus had every right to place Himself above common man. And we are His servants. But we can't serve if we're disengaged from, unaware of, or avoiding others.

Follow your Master's lead. Walk with other people and seek out ways to love them.

Action Point #1

Look at the people around you on the bridge of life. Are you walking *among* them or *with* them? Make an impression on someone that lasts longer than your ten-minute visit to the bridge. Let those in your sphere of influence see Christ through how you show love. Remove any pretense that you're above anyone else.

Action Point #2

Come back to the bridge at night and watch the street lights reflect on the river. As you admire the city, ask God to help you "walk" among others, showing love and being a servant. Ask Him to show you what that looks like.

"Do nothing from selfishness or empty conceit, but with humility of mind regard one another as more important than yourselves; do not merely look out for your own personal interests, but also for the interests of others.

Have this attitude in yourselves which was also in Christ Jesus, who, although He existed in the form of God, did not regard equality with God a thing to be grasped, but emptied Himself, taking the form of a bond-servant, and being made in the likeness of men.

Being found in appearance as a man, He humbled Himself by becoming obedient to the point of death, even death on a cross" (Philippians 2:3-8).

Souvenirs · Stamps · Notes

Girolamo Savonarola

Several things must take place for dynamite to explode. A match must be struck, the fuse must be lit, and the spark has to follow a path until it reaches the powder for detonation. In the same way, the explosion of the Reformation started long before Luther nailed his thesis to the church door in Wittenberg, Germany.

Faithful men and women lit the match and carried the spark of truth. The man who carried the spark the last few inches was Girolamo Savonarola. (Say that name five times fast!)

In fact, the Reformation could have started in Florence if Savonarola had not been executed in the Piazza della Signoria.

Look at the seal on the ground next to the Fountain of Neptune and you'll find Savonarola's name. He died in this square nineteen years before Luther's hammer drove the nail into the door of Castle Church.

As radical as his preaching was, Savonarola called the Florentines to live according to God's Word, and spiritual revival spread throughout the city. The cravings of materialism once held by the Florentines transformed into a thirst for the Bible. Citizens threw away their materialistic idols of worship, tarot cards, and pagan books and literature, burning them at what was called the Bonfire of the Vanities.

Meanwhile, one of the most brutal popes in Catholic Church history set his sights on the bold Dominican monk reformer. Pope Borgia, aka Alexander VI, made the *Sopranos* look like kindergarten bullies. In mob-like fashion, he bribed his way into the papacy, sold indulgences and Cardinal seats for money, sired at least twelve illegitimate children, and brutally murdered anyone who spoke out against him. Corruption within the church reached a sickening pinnacle, and Savonarola held Pope Borgia accountable.

The pope offered Savonarola a bribe to silence him. He refused. The pope excommunicated Savonarola from the church and had him arrested, then brought him to trial and tried to force him to recant. Again, he refused. On May 23, 1498, he was tortured and burned at the stake.

Amazingly, Savonarola's influence never died. His sacrifice was not in vain. Almost every word of his preaching and writing was printed and distributed. Some of his letters arrived into the hands of Martin Luther. Historians speculate whether or not Luther was inspired by Savonarola's teachings. Nevertheless, Luther carried the spark and changed the world.

All believers are connected to a supernatural power that cannot be silenced—the power of God's truth. Because of Girolamo Savonarola, the last few inches of the fuse held its spark. God used him to springboard Luther and ignite a reformation that would change the world.

Action Point #1

As you walk within the square, try to picture what it was like for Savonarola to be on display before the crowd and stand up for his faith. How hard it must have been! Ask God to give you that kind of boldness and courage to stand by the truth of the Bible.

Action Point #2

Pray for those who still suffer throughout the world for their faith in Jesus Christ. In this century, there have been more Christians martyred for their faith than in the last nineteen centuries combined.[3] Praise God for our freedom and pray for those who sacrifice their lives and families every day.

> "But we have this treasure [Jesus Christ] in earthen vessels, so that the surpassing greatness of the power will be of God and not from ourselves; we are afflicted in every way, but not crushed; perplexed, but not despairing; persecuted, but not forsaken; struck down, but not destroyed; always carrying about in the body the dying of Jesus, so that the life of Jesus also may be manifested in our body" (2 Corinthians 4:7-10).

ROME

Souvenirs › Stamps › Notes

Colosseum

One sure way to pick a fight with a Colosseum guide is to argue that Christians were martyred inside the arena.

Skeptics claim martyrdom never happened. Yet a collection of historical documents in the Acts of Martyrs contain eyewitness accounts of men who died for their faith inside the Colosseum.

The most reliable story is about Ignatius, the first recorded martyr who lost his life in the Colosseum for his faith in Jesus Christ.

Ignatius's death sentence began twenty-seven years after the opening ceremony of the Colosseum. Legend says he was the child Jesus presented to His disciples when He said to them, "Truly I say to you, unless you are converted and become like children, you will not enter the kingdom of heaven" (Matthew 18:3).

Whether or not Ignatius's boyhood legend is true, we know he served as the Bishop of Antioch, modern-day Antakya, Turkey, which was one of the largest cities in the Roman Empire. He was also a disciple of the apostle John.

In a discourse with Emperor Trajan in AD 107, Ignatius declared that Jesus Christ, the one crucified and who rose from the dead, resided inside his heart. And he proclaimed Jesus to be the one and only true God.

Ignatius's statement fueled the popular anti-Christian sentiment circulating throughout the Empire. Trajan, known to be easily persuaded by his people, could not show the weakness to allow such blasphemy. He'd make the bishop an example to all who followed Jesus. He shipped Ignatius to Rome to die in the Colosseum by the claws of lions.

Ignatius leapt for joy because he was allowed to suffer for the Lord. He wrote letters to the Christians in Rome, pleading with them to not intercede in prayer for his rescue. He didn't want his crown of death to be taken from him. Being considered worthy to die for Christ gave him unexplainable happiness.

In a letter he wrote on the way to Rome five months before he died, he said, "Let me be the food of the beasts; let me come thus to the possession of God. I am the wheat of Jesus Christ; I must therefore be ground and broken by the teeth of wild beasts, that I may become His pure and spotless bread."[4]

On December 20, 107, Roman guards escorted Ignatius from his prison on Palatine Hill to the arena. He stood on the sand-covered floor of the Colosseum in front of fifty thousand spectators and addressed the Emperor. "Romans who witness my death, do not think I am condemned on account of any crime or bad action; it is permitted that I may come to God, whom I desire with an insatiable desire."[5]

The gates opened and unleashed two lions onto the kneeling man, and the beasts devoured him until there was no more.

For three more centuries, crowds of some fifty thousand Romans gathered in the arena to watch similar scenes, along with reenacted Roman battles, never-before-seen exotic animals, gladiatorial fights, and executions. In other arenas throughout the Empire, slaves, paid gladiators, Christians, and prisoners of war died at the applause and hearty approval of thousands.

What finally brought the Colosseum to an end?

One historical account, written by Theodoret, the Bishop of Cyrrhus in Syria, tells the story of a monk named Telemachus who died in a "stadium." In AD 400, the monk traveled to Rome from the east. When he saw the gladiatorial battles, he entered the arena and pleaded with the warriors to stop fighting. An angry mob retaliated by stoning him to death. Some believe his sacrifice helped end the brutal games in the Colosseum.

Finding evidence for the validity of the Colosseum's recorded history can be as nebulous as understanding how the Romans filled and emptied the Colosseum with water in order to reenact Roman sea battles.

If the walls of the Colosseum could speak, we'd all know the truth. The stones would surely recount stories of the blood-and-sweat-covered hands of the Jewish slaves who built the stadium and of how the Romans traded treasures from within the Jewish temple in exchange for the construction materials. (See chapter on the Arch of Titus.)

Since the days of the Colosseum, statistics regarding Christian persecution have grown to shocking numbers. More Christians are martyred today than in all other centuries combined.[6] The skeleton of the Colosseum and other ancient arenas remind us not only of those who've died for their faith in the one true God, but also of man's depravity. The wickedness that led Emperors Nero, Trajan, and others to persecute people exists within us—it's called sin.

If we lived two thousand years ago, who's to say we wouldn't be sitting among the fifty thousand watching the entertainment?

Praise God for sending His Son to be our Savior from sin. None of us is free without Christ. When you think about the Colosseum, let it be a reminder of all those who even today stand for Jesus in the face of adversity. No matter the cost.

Action Point #1

As you walk inside the Colosseum, find the cross. Pope Benedict XIV placed the cross on the balcony where the emperors used to sit to watch the games. The crucifix represents all Christian martyrs throughout the world.

Take the time to pray for the thousands of Christians who are under persecution today for their faith in Jesus Christ.

Action Point #2

Find a place to sit or stand on the second level and observe the arena. Picture the Colosseum in AD 80. Envision all kinds of entertainment taking place in front of you.

Over time, entertainment can build passivity toward evil. Guard against becoming callous and comfortable with things you once found offensive and wrong. Use Scripture as the lens through which you view entertainment and the world. Ask God if there is any offensive way in you that needs to be taken care of before Him.

(See Psalm 139:24)

"What blessings await you when people hate you and exclude you and mock you and curse you as evil because you follow the Son of Man. When that happens, be happy! Yes, leap for joy! For a great reward awaits you in heaven. And remember, their ancestors treated the ancient prophets that same way" (Luke 6: 22-23 NLT).

"Therefore we do not lose heart, but though our outer man is decaying, yet our inner man is being renewed day by day. For momentary, light affliction is producing for us an eternal weight of glory far beyond all comparison, while we look not at the things which are seen, but at the things which are not seen: for the things which are seen are temporal, but the things which are not seen are eternal" (2 Corinthians 4:16-18).

Souvenirs › Stamps › Notes

Arch of Titus
Foro Romano Roma
AD 81

On the day before Jesus' betrayal, He made a prophecy regarding the temple of Jerusalem. After His disciples pointed out how beautiful the temple was, Jesus said, "Truly I say to you, not one stone here will be left upon another, which will not be torn down" (Matthew 24:2).

His comment didn't exactly win "popular prediction of the year" with the Jews.

How could their beautiful temple, one of the wonders of the ancient world and Judaism's biggest shrine, be destroyed? For forty-six years, since 20 BC, the building had been under construction by Herod, who trained priests to become builders and overseers of the project so the structure would remain holy. Over the years, people adorned the sanctuary walls with precious stones. They donated golden statues and priceless treasures as a symbol of their vows to God (Luke 21:5).

In AD 70, Emperor Vespasian's son Titus fulfilled Jesus' prophecy.

In order to crush a Jewish rebellion, Titus brought an army to Jerusalem and held the city under siege. For two years, nothing went into the city and nothing came out.

Starvation led to some Jews eating anything they could find to stay alive, including animal corpses, clothing, and grass. Despite the overwhelming odds, the Jews defended until the very end.

By the time the Romans breached the city walls, any of Titus's inclinations to spare the Jews' precious temple were completely rejected. The war had cost his army too many casualties. A totally destroyed temple would mean legitimate victory.

Fire spread from the outer court into the temple. The Romans attacked with no mercy, killing everyone, young and old. The screams of the dying Jews echoed off the surrounding mountains.

As the flames subsided, Titus ordered his men to level the entire city so that no future generations would believe such a temple even existed.

Titus's brother, Domitian, built the Arch of Titus to commemorate the victory. On the inside of the arch, the builder depicted the Roman army hauling away the menorah.

Did the things prophesied in the Bible actually happen? Yes! The Arch of Titus is a tangible reminder that God always does what He says He'll do. We can touch the evidence of prophecy.

God will always fulfill His promises. Fortunately for us, along with the promises of pain and destruction due to sin, the Bible is packed full of assurances that give us hope.

When we trust God with all our hearts, He makes our paths straight (Proverbs 3:5–6). When we don't worry about money or possessions but seek God instead, He provides for our needs (Matthew 6:24–34). When we obey God and revere Him, He discloses Himself to us (John 14:21). And most important, when we surrender our lives to Jesus, He gives us eternal life (1 John 5:11–12). Praise God for His inability to break a promise!

Action Point #1

Find a place to sit within the Roman Forum. Think about a time when one of God's promises rang true in your life. Recall some Bible verses you claimed and remember how He fulfilled each one. Thank Him for being faithful, for being someone you can always depend on. Ask Him to give you courage to trust in Him daily.

Action Point #2

Perhaps you need a promise from God right now. There are a few on the next page to get you started.

Keep your head up, even if you can't see God's promises in your life right now. Remember, God had to tell Joshua to "be strong and courageous (Joshua 1:6–9)" four times in one sitting. Like Joshua, we need to hear encouragement over and over.

About forty years passed before Jesus' words were fulfilled through Titus. Most of us won't have to wait that long to see God's promises come to light in our lives. But even if we do, His Word will never fail.

PURITY *Psalm 119:9*

DISCOURAGEMENT *Isaiah 40:29-31*

PURPOSE *Philippians 1:6*

ANGER *Proverbs 25:28*

FORGIVENESS *1 John 1:9*

CONFUSION *Romans 8:28*

MONEY *Hebrews 13:5-6*

SHAME *Romans 8:1*

"The grass withers, the flower fades, but the word of our God stands forever" (Isaiah 40:8).

"How can a young man keep his way pure? By keeping it according to Your word. With all my heart I have sought You. Do not let me wander from Your commandments. Your word I have treasured in my heart, that I may not sin against You. Blessed are You, O Lord; teach me Your statutes. With my lips I have told of all the ordinances of Your mouth. I have rejoiced in the way of Your testimonies, as much as in all riches. I will meditate on Your precepts and regard Your ways. I shall delight in Your statutes; I shall not forget Your word" (Psalm 119:9-16).

Souvenirs › Stamps › Notes

Mamertine Prison

Via dei Falegnami, I-00186 Roma
640-616 BC

The apostle Paul spent his last days in the damp well of Mamertine Prison. While he awaited execution ordered by Emperor Nero, Paul penned a second letter to his friend and partner in the service of Jesus Christ. Though originally intended for Timothy, Paul's words resonate with every believer.

The last words of a dying man are powerful. Each word is chosen with care as the clock ticks off the remaining seconds of his life. There's no time for explanation. Vocabulary must be succinct. Language laced with substance.

And so we listen.

The ink of Paul's pen bled with exhortation to all who believed in the Messiah. Listen to the powerful words of God spoken through a dying man.

"I solemnly charge you in the presence of God and of Christ Jesus who is to judge the living and the dead, and by His appearing and His kingdom: preach the word; be ready in season and out of season; reprove, rebuke, exhort, with great patience and instruction.

For the time will come when they will not endure sound doctrine; but wanting to have their ears tickled, they will accumulate for themselves teachers in accordance to their own desires, and will turn away their ears from the truth and will turn aside to myths.

But you, be sober in all things, endure hardship,
do the work of an evangelist, fulfill your minis-
try. For I am already being poured out as a drink
offering, and the time of my departure has come.
I have fought the good fight, I have finished the
course, I have kept the faith; in the future there
is laid up for me the crown of righteousness,
which the Lord, the righteous Judge, will award to
me on that day; and not only to me, but also to
all who have loved His appearing"
(2 Timothy 4:1-8).

Action Point #1

Find a place to sit outside the prison. How are you doing with Paul's encouragement? Are you fighting the good fight or sitting on the sidelines? Where are you spiritually? Examine your heart with God right now.

Action Point #2

What do you think your last words before you die will be? Hard to say, since none of us knows when our time is going to be up. How should we live if we're not sure which moment will be our last? Be careful what you say to others or what you complain about.

Decide to encourage and lift someone up with your words. Do it now. Make every minute of your life count.

Souvenirs › Stamps › Notes

Pantheon

Piazza Della Rotonda 1-00186 Roma

AD 125

The Pantheon is a reflection of how the Romans used ingenuity to show off greatness. Caesars claimed themselves divine, and Emperor Hadrian was no exception. His design and construction of the Pantheon displayed his "divinity" to the world.

The ceiling's well-known Oculus allows in the only source of light, and recent theories state the Oculus may have served as a sundial. Twice a year during the equinox—when the center of the sun is at the Earth's equator—as Emperor Hadrian entered through the Pantheon's bronze doors, the sun would shine on him like a spotlight through the Oculus. The Roman sun god, Sol Invictus, would illuminate Hadrian's glory.

A careful look at the outside of the building shows how his search for perfection fell short. Walk to the west side of the building and stand on the street called Salita de Crescenzi. From this vantage point, take a closer look at the external part of the Pantheon. Notice the V-shaped outline above the roof of the porch. The offset has baffled engineers for centuries because the porch looks as if it was meant to be higher. Historians theorize that perhaps the Romans had reached the limits of their ingenuity. The columns, though originally meant to be higher, were too short when they arrived from Egypt. So the Romans' attempt at perfection missed the mark.

It's pretty impressive that Hadrian built the largest unsupported concrete dome in the world, which inspired countless buildings through the centuries, and created an Oculus that possibly served as a sundial. Many people believe the Pantheon is one of the top wonders of the world. But in the end, it's just a less-than-perfect building.

Most people are excellent at putting on a facade that makes them look good. We do it all the time. We work hard to look perfect in front of others. Even before God, we try to show how great we are through moral actions, prayer, and the things we sacrifice. But God sees past it all. We are all sinners in desperate need of His mercy. Just like Hadrian, we'll always fall short of perfection.

That's what is so amazing about grace. The fact that God, in His divine reason, reached down and chose sinners like us and covered us with His holiness. There is nothing we can do to earn His favor. He sees who we really are, and even though our hearts are ugly, He loves us and rescued us.

Action Point #1

Stand beneath the Oculus. Compare man's accomplishments with the blue sky above. God has outdone us all. If you have a relationship with God, praise Him for saving you. If you don't know Him, ask someone to tell you about what He did for you, and read the Reality section in the back of this book.

Action Point #2

What is your motive for being perfect at something? Is your motivation like Hadrian's, so that others will look up to, adore, and sing praises to you? Or do you strive to be excellent in all you do so that you may bring God glory? If it's the former, ask God to change your heart and perspective. Be excellent and influence the world. But do it for God.

"We're all sin-infected, sin-contaminated. Our best efforts are grease-stained rags. We dry up like autumn leaves—sin-dried, we're blown off by the wind" (Isaiah 64:6 MSG).

"But God, being rich in mercy, because of His great love with which He loved us, even when we were dead in our transgressions, made us alive together with Christ (by grace you have been saved), and raised us up with Him, and seated us with Him in the heavenly places in Christ Jesus, so that in the ages to come He might show the surpassing riches of His grace in kindness towar us in Christ Jesus" (Ephesians 2:4-7).

Souvenirs · Stamps · Notes

Piazza Navona

Piazza Navona, built upon the remains of Domitian's athletic stadium, still captures the legacy of competition. The combative story of two master architects, Francesco Borromini and Gianlorenzo Bernini, lies within the *Fontana dei Quattro Fiumi*—Fountain of the Four Rivers.

Borromini and Bernini defined Baroque architecture. Almost every breathtaking fountain, cathedral, and piazza in Rome bears the fingerprints of one of these artists.

The conflict began when Borromini worked on a highly coveted project in Rome: the design of St. Peter's Basilica. He worked under the mentorship of his uncle, Carlo Moderno. Borromini had hopes of one day succeeding his master and becoming the lead architect on the project.

When Moderno died, the time came for Pope Urbana VIII to elect the new lead architect. Borromini probably rehearsed his victory speech. Much to his surprise, he was not chosen. Instead, a more well-known artist—better dressed, more personable, and a good friend of the dear pope—received the title.

Bernini was chosen as lead architect at age twenty-four. From that day on, his contempt for Borromini, which was returned in kind, fueled and propelled the two architects into a lifelong competition against each other.

After Pope Urbana died, Borromini received a second chance to step out from Bernini's shadow. To Borromini's fortune, Pope Innocent favored him over Bernini. Around 1647, the new pope commissioned Borromini to sculpt a fountain for the Piazza Navona. The sculptor presented his idea of a fountain representing the four rivers of the known world: Europe's Danube, India's Ganges, Africa's Nile, and South America's Plata.

Once again, thanks to friends in high places, Bernini found a way to slip his interpretation of the project in front of the pope at just the right time. To everyone's surprise, the pope awarded Bernini the job.

Bernini completed the fountain using Borromini's idea of representing the four great rivers in four statues.

Take a close look at the statues and the church alongside the piazza—St. Agnese, which was built by Borromini. Notice that not one of the four statues is looking at the church. In fact, the Plata, on the northwest corner, is holding out a hand, rearing back as though in preparation to brace himself if the church should fall. The Nile, on the northeast corner, pulls a shroud over his eyes.

Some call the mockery coincidence because the church of St. Agnese was rebuilt one year after the fountain was finished. But perhaps Bernini knew what he was doing to scorn his rival.

How would have you acted if you were one of these men? Imagine being in a close race to be declared the absolute best in the world in your chosen field—and then finishing second. You'd be angry too.

Everyone loves a good rivalry—especially when both competitors, equally matched in skill, share a history of tension. At what point does competition go too far and instead of bringing out the best in someone, brings out the worst?

We need to be careful not to take competition too seriously. When our pride flares, so do our insecurities. We're more successful when we take what God has given us, do our best, and let Him take care of the rest.

Even in competition, we need to love others. Within the realm of contest, wrapping our minds around loving is difficult. The concept seems foreign. However, those who have found success in loving while competing realize how much that mind-set helps keep their worst from getting in the way.

Action Point #1

Are you a competitive person? Do you flaunt your abilities and parade your talents? We could all use some humility when showcasing our skills. After all, they came from God. Don't abuse what He's given you. Instead, use your gifts to point people to the one who gave them to you. That's love. Instead of boasting, let God raise you up.

Action Point #2

Is there someone you've been competing against who always seems to gain the edge? Do you sometimes feel like Borromini, competing in the shadow of someone else? Don't let these circumstances cheapen what God has given you. Don't believe the lie that your status in the world matters. God made you the way you are and He knew every detail before you were even born (Psalm 139). He doesn't make mistakes. He is perfection. So lift your head—you were made exactly as you were supposed to be.

Stop focusing on yourself. Instead, go "sculpt" something great for God. Experience the joy in watching how He uses your talents and draws others to Himself by means of your gifts.

"An arrogant man stirs up strife, but he who trusts in the Lord will prosper. He who trusts in his own heart is a fool, but he who walks wisely will be delivered" (Proverbs 28:25-26).

"If you have been foolish in exalting yourself or if you have plotted evil, put your hand on your mouth. For the churning of milk produces butter, and pressing the nose brings forth blood: so the churning of anger produces strife"
(Proverbs 30:32-33).

Souvenirs › Stamps › Notes

St. Peter's Basilica

Viale Giulio Cesare (Angolo Via Barletta), 62 00192 Roma
AD 1506-1615

St. Peter's Basilica tells the story of a master architect who lived a full life and never wasted an ounce of his God-given talent.

Over a span of more than one hundred years, the premier artists of the Renaissance and Baroque eras set their designs and chisels to work on rebuilding the new St. Peter's Basilica. Among its many architects was a seventy-two-year-old man who had just finished painting *The Last Judgment* in the Sistine Chapel. A tired man, labeled out of his mind and finished, his glory days were long gone.

In spite of those criticisms, Michelangelo Buonarroti accepted the position of lead architect in 1546. Even though Pope Paul III practically wrestled the old artist into acquiring the position, Michelangelo made his motivation clear on what would become his greatest challenge yet.

He wasn't doing this for money. Michelangelo refused payment. Nor did he desire more fame. If anything, this master artist deserved a lavish retirement and a chance to put away his sculpting tools and paintbrushes. He could probably hear the waves of the Mediterranean rippling against the shores of Sardinia. Warm sand. Clean ocean air. All beckoning him to a life of relaxation.

No one would blame him for retiring. Weren't his creations *David*, *Pietà*, and *Moses* enough? What about his work in the Sistine Chapel: *The Creation of Adam* and *The Last Judgment*?

But Michelangelo resisted the enticement to quit. In a letter to his nephew, he shared his motivation. "Many believe—and I believe—that I have been designated for this work by God. In spite of my old age, I do not want to give it up; I work out of love for God and I put all my hope in Him."[7]

Michelangelo knew his calling, even until the end. He recognized the years of experience God had given him, and he used everything he'd learned, pouring it into one final job. His expertise in managing a project helped him tweak the original design for the Basilica produced by Donato Bramante.

Michelangelo's integrity gave him authority to oversee the project's exorbitant finances. Furthermore, his humility allowed him to engineer the dome of St. Peter after seeing Brunelleschi's dome on the Florence cathedral and acknowledging its greatness.

Michelangelo accepted the talents God gave him, multiplied them, and never stopped using them.

Legend says the apostle Peter was crucified upside down on the site of St. Peter's Basilica for his faith in Jesus Christ.

He too knew his calling—to serve and love Christ and His church until the end. And he followed it.

One of the saddest things in life is wasted talent. Yet we often see it in both the younger and the older generations—God-given gifts and abilities never used for any significance. How tragic!

Nobody would've pointed a finger at Michelangelo if he'd refused to take the lead role on the Basilica. But he recognized his talents as gifts and used them to impact the world. He continued on until the end out of a love for God. A way of saying "Thank You" to God for his talents.

Action Point #1

As you stand in St. Peter's Square and view the dome, consider what God-given talents and abilities you possess. Ask God to show you how to use them to impact the world and bring glory to Him. Commit to never give up until you see Him face-to-face.

"Work willingly at whatever you do, as though you were working for the Lord rather than for people. Remember that the Lord will give you an inheritance as your reward, and that the Master you are serving is Christ" (Colossians 3:23 NLT).

Action Point #2

Find Michelangelo's *Pietà* inside the Basilica. This Italian word means "pity" or "mercy." The sculpture depicts Mary mourning over her son, Jesus the Messiah. Michelangelo was twenty-four years old when he finished the masterpiece.

Use your camera to zoom in and view the inscription on Mary's sash. It reads, "Michelangelo Buonarroti, Florentine, made this." Michelangelo had overheard a pilgrim declare that another artist had created the sculpture. That night, Michelangelo's anger led him to chisel his own name onto the statue. After his temper cooled, he realized his decision was a mistake and vowed never to sign another piece of his work.

"A fool always loses his temper, but a wise man holds it back" (Proverbs 29:11).

"Do you see a man skilled in his work? He will stand before kings; He will not stand before obscure men" (Proverbs 22:29).

JOURNAL

Day 1

Something God showed me or reminded
me today:

Something I experienced today that I don't
want to forget:

Day 2

Out of everything I saw today, what transformed me?

How am I different today than yesterday?

Day 3

My favorite part of today was:

When I was seeing the sights today, who did I wish was with me?

Day 4

Something about life I never realized:

ı

One thing I will tell about when I get back:

Day 5

What I learned about myself today:

How can I love the people I'm surrounded by on this trip (either on the team or locals)?

Day 6

How has my view of other people in different parts of the world changed?

What kind of sacrifices were made for me to be here?

Day 7

One thing I learned today that will help me live differently when I return home:

Out of the stories I've learned so far, which one could I use as a tool to tell others about Jesus? Who needs to hear His story?

Day 8

These attributes about God really stood
out to me today:

How did my realtionship with Jesus grow
during my trip?

Reality
Your Life

You are now en route to reality. No more tours. No more sightseeing. No more multiple-mile walks through foreign streets. You're headed for home, friends, and a big, juicy American hamburger.

Once the airplane hits the runway, life will kick in and you'll be back in the fast lane. School, responsibilities, and work are all waiting for you—requiring decisions you must make. Every day.

Before you hit reality, let me ask you a question. What matters most in life?

Where I attend college?

Doesn't even come close.

Who my friends are?

Nope.

Where I will live?

Not quite.

Who I'm going to marry and how many kids we'll have?

Good guess. But still not there. Let me help you out.

Your relationship with God matters most.

That's it?

That's everything.

I think I have a relationship with Him. I go to church and pray sometimes. I'm a good person.

Well, I have good and bad news for you.

The bad news?

The bad news is that since the day you were born, you began to die because you have a terminal disease. You've had this infection longer than you can remember. The disease is in everybody and it is called sin.

"For all have sinned and fallen short of the glory of God" (Romans 3:23).

Because of sin, you are also spiritually dead, and therefore separated from God. "The wages of sin is death" (Romans 6:23). Because He is holy, God can have no part with sin (Psalm 5:4). The Bible even says we are His enemies without the cure (Romans 5:10).

But I think God knows the good things I do. Isn't that the cure?

There is only one cure for your disease, and being good is not the antidote.

Have you ever told a lie? Stolen? Cheated? One time is all it takes to be a liar or a thief (James 2:10). And have you ever wondered just how good is good enough? Those times you went to church, gave to the poor, and did your best were all good, but they will never be enough for you to be made right with God. What if after you died, God said you would've made it into heaven if only you had done one more good thing?

In the section about the Pantheon we learned how God views our righteous deeds. You'll never reach the perfection He requires. Not only are you a dead man living on earth separated from God (Ephesians 2:1), but you'll also be separated from God for eternity when you die.

If there's nothing I can do to have a relationship with Him, then how can anybody say they know Him? How can I be made right with God?

Here's the good news. Instead of leaving us to find our own cure, God has given us the answer.

The Bible records a time when Jesus' disciples, Paul and Silas were beaten and put in jail for following Jesus. The magistrates charged the jailer with a specific duty—to make sure the prisoners did not escape. The jailer took extra measures to obey his orders. He threw the disciples into the inner prison and secured them in stocks probably hoping their confinement would also shut their mouths from worshipping God. At midnight, a massive earthquake broke the foundations of the prison. Every cell door and every shackle broke free.

The jailer awoke, saw the destruction, and trembled in fear. He had failed. His prisoners had most likely escaped. Now he was at the mercy of both his leaders and God. The punishment would mean death by his superiors. With nowhere to turn, he took out his sword and set the blade against his chest to take his own life.

"Stop! We are all still here!" Paul cried out to him, just in time.

The jailer ran into the disciples' cell, fell at their feet, and asked, "What must I do to be saved?" In other words, "How can I receive mercy from this awesome God of yours? I need Him to save me from death!"

Their response: "Believe in the Lord Jesus and you will be saved" (Acts 16:31).

That's the answer.

It took an act of God to awaken the jailer both physically and spiritually. When he awoke and saw the destruction of his prison, he saw his own reflection. He was in trouble, with no hope of mercy for his failure. God broke Him. As the blade rested against his skin, he must have wondered about life after death more than ever. What was on the other side? Was eternity real?

Paul offered him an alternative—the same alternative available to you. It's grace. Out of God's love for us, He sent His Son to pay the penalty for our sin and die in our place in the man named Jesus. Out of love, Jesus took on the sins of the world, died, and came back to life three days later. He defeated the very penalty of sin: death.

You cannot afford to put off eternity until later. Tomorrow may be too late. Everything else can wait. In fact, you can start living out the benefits of knowing God today once you settle your standing with Him. You'll no longer be a slave to sin. He will give you His Spirit to live inside you and to guide you in every matter of life.

Before "reality" gets in the way, take care of the true reality. Trust in Jesus to heal your disease and connect you with God. Then, by knowing Him, you will experience freedom—a new relationship with Him.

Action Point #1

Wherever you are, stop what you're doing and settle what matters most in life. Trust in Jesus right now to forgive you from the penalty of sin. Talk to God and pour out your heart to Him. Admit you are a sinner. Repent, grab hold of the only cure for your disease, and commit your life to Him.

Now go tell someone the decision you made. Find people who follow Jesus to help you learn more about God's story and how you fit into it. Get a Bible, read it to find out more about God, and find a church that teaches the Bible. Your life will never be the same.

Action Point #2

Maybe you don't buy into this right now. Only God can shake you from your sleep. You need Him to break your world and bring you to reality. Ask Him to make Himself known to you. If you're not there yet, be honest with Him and ask Him to help you with your unbelief. This life and the next depend on it.

"But God demonstrates His own love toward us, in that while we were yet sinners, Christ died for us" (Romans 5:8).

"God has given us eternal life, and this life is in His Son. He who has the Son has the life [heaven]: he who does not have the Son of God does not have the life [his destiny is hell]. These things I have written to you who believe in the name of the Son of God, so that you may know you have eternal life" (1 John 5:11-13).

Notes

1. Michaelangelo Buonaroti, Italian Painter, Sculptor (1475–1564)

2. Giorgio Vasari, *Vasari's Lives of the Artists*, translated by Mrs. Jonathan Foster (Mineola: Dover Publications, Inc, 2005), 197.

3. K.P. Yohannan, *Revolution in World Missions: One Man's Journey to Change A Generation* (Carrollton, TX: GFA Books, 2004), 144. Originally published in David B. Barrett and Todd M. Johnson, *World Christian Trends AD 30–AD 2200* (Pasadena, California: William Carey Library, 2001), 32.

4. Rev. A. J. O'Reilly, *The Martyrs of the Coliseum; or Historical Records of the Great Amphitheatre of Ancient Rome* (London: Burns, Oates, & Company, 1871), 45–46.

5. Ibid., 51.

6. Yohannan, *Revolution in World Missions*, 32.

7. Ray Doliner and Benjamin Belch, *The Sistine Secrets: Michelangelo's Forbidden Messages in the Heart of the Vatican* (New York: Harper Collins, 2008), Page 273.

Historical research for *Santa Maria del Fiore* was taken from:

King, Ross. *Brunelleschi's Dome: How a Renaissance Genius Reinvented Architecture*. New York, NY: Bloomsbury, 2013. Print.

BE TRANSFORMED

I hope you enjoyed *The Christian's Travel Journal for Italy*. Please be so kind as to leave feedback on the journal wherever you purchased it online. I am grateful for your comments.

Future books coming soon!

The Christian's Travel Journal for Paris

The Christian's Travel Journal for London

The Christian's Travel Journal for Washington DC